To Trish, my future wife: without her this book would have been impossible. R.C.

Special thanks to: Kenworth Truck Company, Navistar International Corporation, Fiat-Allis, Eldorado Motor Corporation, Fleetwood Enterprises Corporation, the New York City Fire Department, and the National Aeronautics and Space Administration (NASA).

THE BIG BOOK OF REAL
TRUCKS

BARNES &NOBLE BOOKS NEW YORK

by Walter Retan
illustrated by Richard Courtney

here are about 34 million trucks in the United States—one truck for every seven people. That is a lot of trucks! Trucks come in many shapes, sizes, and styles, and do all kinds of jobs. They carry food from farms to supermarkets. They transport manufactured goods from factories to stores. They deliver gasoline to filling stations and heating oil to homes.

The army uses trucks. The postal service uses trucks. Even milk is delivered by truck. In fact, today 75 percent of all the freight moved in the United States travels by truck.

Although people started using them as early as the 1890s, trucks did not become really popular until after World War I, in the 1920s. When you see pictures of some of the early trucks you can understand why. They looked like horse-drawn wagons—without the horses—or like Model T cabs pulling hay wagons.

After World War I the designs and the engines steadily improved. Door-to-door delivery by trucks became more and more popular. In 1925 alone, half a million trucks were manufactured.

Today trucking is one of the most important businesses in the United States. Some of the trucks that make that possible are shown in this book.

Trucks can be divided into three main groups:

PICKUP TRUCK **PANEL TRUCK** **TOW TRUCK**

Light Trucks • These include pickups and panel trucks, some light vans and tow trucks. The gross weight of light trucks is less than 10,000 pounds. (By gross weight we mean the total weight of the truck with its load.) Most light trucks have gasoline engines. Manufacturers have begun to make a few with diesel engines. They burn oil instead of gas.

MULTISTOP TRUCK **BOTTLER** **VAN**

Medium Trucks • These are higher and wider than light trucks. They are usually used for commercial or business purposes and include bottle trucks, vans, and multistop-delivery trucks. Like light trucks, medium trucks are one-piece, straight trucks (as opposed to two-piece tractor trailers). Many of them use diesel fuel. The gross weight of medium trucks is from 10,000 to 20,000 pounds.

DUMP TRUCK **TRACTOR AND SEMITRAILER** **READY-MIX CONCRETE TRUCK**

Heavy Trucks • These trucks are sometimes broken into two groups—light heavy and heavy heavy. The first group weighs from 20,000 to 26,000 pounds. The second group weighs more than 26,000 pounds. Almost all heavy trucks have diesel engines. Dump trucks, tractor trailers, tank trucks, and concrete trucks are all heavy trucks.

Tractor-trailers are the most popular kind of truck for hauling heavy loads of freight long distances. They are often called big rigs or 18-wheelers. The front part is the *tractor*. It contains the engine, the cab where the driver sits, and the fuel tanks.

The *trailer* is the part that carries the load. Trailers come in many shapes and styles. The most common for carrying freight is the long, box-shaped, enclosed van. Most trailers have no front wheels so they are called semitrailers, or just semis. The trailers usually have 8 wheels. The big, powerful tractors usually have 10 wheels. That is why these big rigs are called 18-wheelers.

Most of the big rigs are powered by diesel engines. A diesel engine has no carburetor or spark plugs. Diesel fuel, which is cheaper than gasoline, is squirted into the cylinders by a fuel pump. The fumes escape through the smokestack. Sometimes there are smokestacks on each side of the cab.

This trailer is a refrigerator van, sometimes called a reefer. It carries food that must be kept cool or frozen. A big refrigeration unit is attached to the front. Special side doors allow unloaders to get into the freezer section, where all the frozen food is stored. The rear section carries fresh, dry food.

There are two kinds of tractors or cabs. One has its engine in front of the cab—like most cars. It is called a "long nose" or "conventional." The engine is easy to reach for repairs.

The other type of cab has a flat front. The engine is placed under the cab. It is called a "snub nose" or a "cab-over-engine" (COE). The snub nose is easier to drive in city traffic.

The snub nose cab can be tilted forward to allow mechanics to get at the engine. A few cabs are made to tilt backward.

Many big cabs have a built-in sleeping section with a bunk and a separate heating unit. Some even have a television set.

A ring-shaped collar with a notch is mounted on a frame over the rear wheels of the tractor. This is called the "fifth wheel." A steel bolt in the trailer floor fits into the notch and locks into place. This connection allows the trailer to twist and turn.

When the semi is not connected to the tractor, the front end rests on metal legs or dolly wheels. These are cranked up when the trailer is attached to the tractor.

On the Road With a Truck Driver

Charlie drives a big rig for Ma's Tasty Fried Chicken, a fast-food chain. Early in the morning he arrives at the distribution center. The dispatcher gives him a logbook. He tells Charlie where he is driving that day, what load he is carrying, and the exact route he is to follow.

Then Charlie goes to the service garage to pick up his tractor. Mechanics have greased and oiled the engine and fixed a rattle that was bothering Charlie. The truck travels up to 400,000 miles a year, so regular servicing is important to prevent breakdowns on the road.

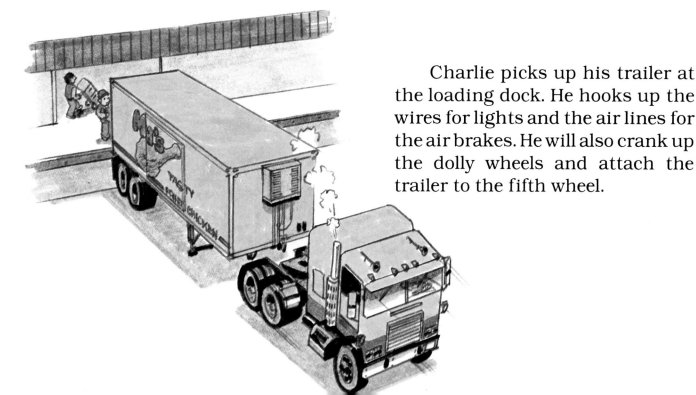

Charlie picks up his trailer at the loading dock. He hooks up the wires for lights and the air lines for the air brakes. He will also crank up the dolly wheels and attach the trailer to the fifth wheel.

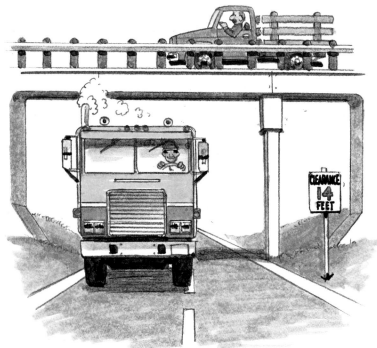

At last Charlie drives out of the distribution center. He must follow the route laid out by the road engineer. The truck can travel only over bridges strong enough to bear its weight. The road engineer also has checked that the truck will clear any bridges under which it has to pass.

While Charlie is driving along the highway, a state officer stops him near a checking station. He has Charlie drive his truck onto a large scale set in the ground. Many states have laws limiting the size of load and length of truck that can be driven on state highways. Charlie's truck passes all the tests.

Back on the road, Charlie picks up his CB (Citizens Band) radio. He talks to a truckdriver friend who is about fifty miles behind him. The friend says, "Watch out. A bird dog passed me about a half-hour ago in a bubble machine." A "bird dog" is CB slang for a police officer looking for speeding drivers. A "bubble machine" is a patrol car with a light and siren.

At 1:00 PM Charlie stops for lunch at a "coffee pot" (trucker slang for a truckers' diner). He notes the time in his logbook before he begins to eat.

After lunch, Charlie gets back on the highway. When he comes to a steep hill, he has to shift gears several times so the truck can go up the hill. Each shift of gears helps the engine pull with more power.

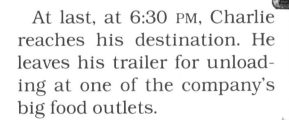

At last, at 6:30 PM, Charlie reaches his destination. He leaves his trailer for unloading at one of the company's big food outlets.

Then Charlie drives his tractor to a motel. It's full, but Charlie doesn't care. He will park in the parking lot and sleep in the bunk in his cab. He has a good dinner, watches television, and then goes to sleep.

In the morning he will pick up his empty trailer and take it to a chicken farm. There he will trade it for another refrigerated trailer already loaded with frozen chickens. He will carry these back to the distribution center.

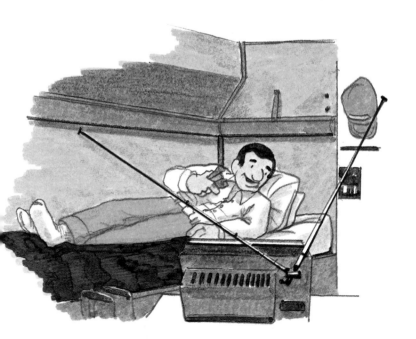

Car Transports are big, powerful tractor-trailers that deliver new cars and small trucks to dealers around the country. The driver picks them up at the factory or from piers where foreign-made cars arrive by ship. In this picture the transport is carrying a load of six new pickup trucks. The trucks are stacked on movable metal racks and secured so they cannot roll off.

To unload the trucks, the driver removes the steel ramps attached to the side of the trailer. The ramps are positioned at the rear of the big truck. Special hydraulic cylinders can raise or lower the metal racks so that they line up with the ramps. By adjusting these perfectly, the driver can drive the small trucks right off the trailer. One of these giant carriers holds as many as ten compact or eight full-size cars.

Tanker Trailers look like huge metal thermos bottles. They can carry as many as 8,000 gallons of gas, oil, or other liquids. (It would take 128,000 eight-ounce lunch box thermos bottles to hold that much liquid!)

This long tanker is delivering gasoline to a filling station. The tank is divided into sections so the truck can carry premium, regular, and unleaded gasoline in separate compartments. The compartments also keep the gasoline from sloshing around when the tank is partly empty.

If the gasoline could shift from side to side, the driver would have a hard time keeping the truck under control when he turned a sharp corner.

The tank is loaded through openings at the top. Most tankers have a ladder on one side or at one end of the tank so the driver can climb up to attach the gas hoses. Different hoses and outlets are used for each kind of gas. The tank is unloaded through openings at the bottom. The gasoline is pulled by gravity or a pump into underground storage tanks.

Tank Trucks also deliver oil from local fuel-supply companies to homes heated by oil furnaces. These trucks are smaller than the 18-wheelers that supply large service stations. The cab and body are usually mounted on a single frame. When the driver stops to make a delivery, he unreels a hose stored at the rear of the truck. The hose is put into a pipe that leads to a tank in the basement of the house. Sometimes the outlet for the pipe is in the sidewalk in front of the house. Then the driver can simply remove a plug and insert the hose. A motor pumps the oil through the hose, and a meter tells how much oil has been delivered.

Moving Vans are perfect for families moving from one home to another. The vans may be semitrailers or one-piece trucks, but the rear half is always shaped like a large, rectangular box. Its doors are airtight to keep out dust and water. Inside the van, heavy padding protects the furniture. There are cardboard cartons, wardrobe boxes, and barrels for packing clothes, books, dishes, and glassware. Rugs are rolled up; mattresses are kept flat. If a family is moving a very long distance, the family car can even be loaded onto the van. Then the family can take a plane or train to the new home.

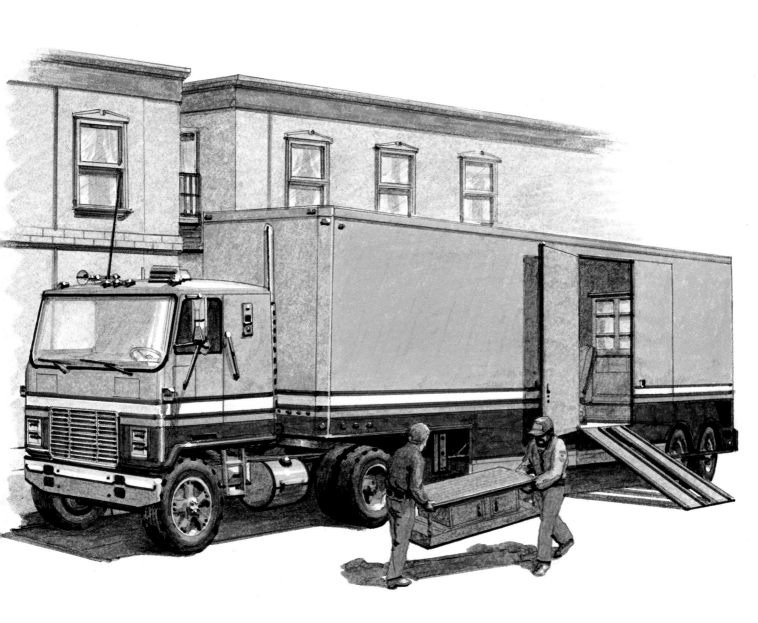

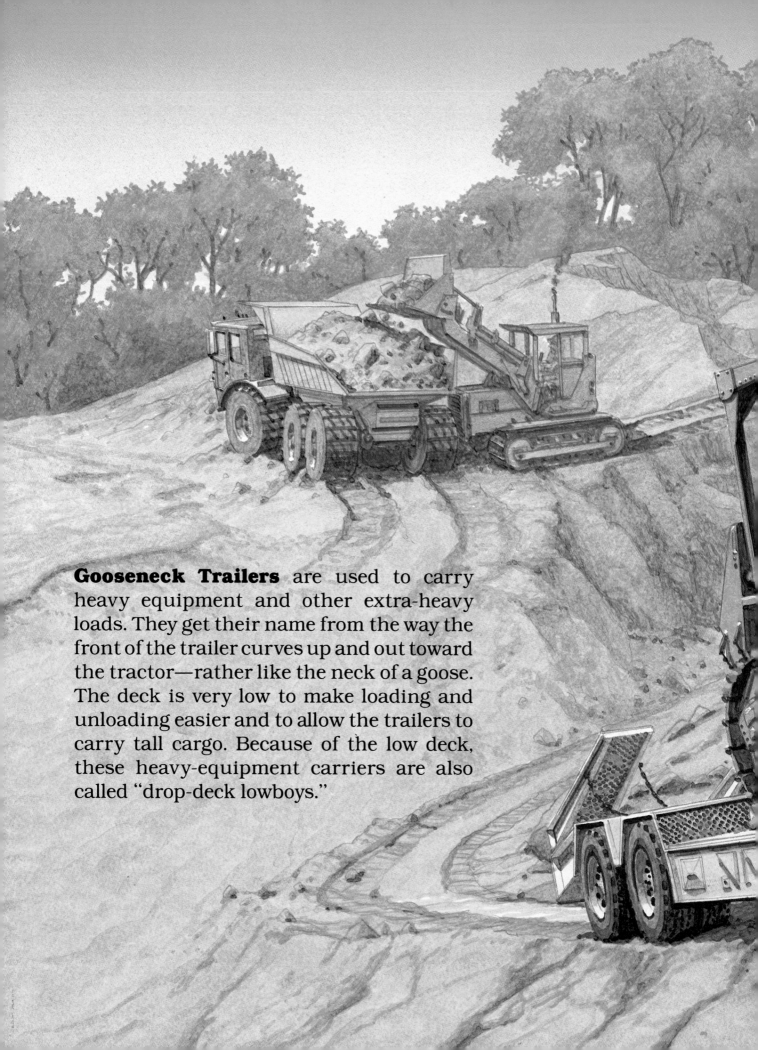

Gooseneck Trailers are used to carry heavy equipment and other extra-heavy loads. They get their name from the way the front of the trailer curves up and out toward the tractor—rather like the neck of a goose. The deck is very low to make loading and unloading easier and to allow the trailers to carry tall cargo. Because of the low deck, these heavy-equipment carriers are also called "drop-deck lowboys."

Here a lowboy carries a bulldozer. Big construction machines like bulldozers move too slowly to travel in regular traffic. They are also so heavy that they could make dents or cracks in the road. The gooseneck trailer is designed to balance all the weight evenly.

Horse Trailers are special tractor-trailers for carrying race horses to the race track. These "rolling stables" may contain as many as fifteen separate stalls. Soft wall-padding protects the horses from injury in case of a sudden jolt. The driver puts food in the stalls so the horses can eat while they ride.

Livestock Trucks carry cattle, hogs, and sheep from farms and ranches to markets and meat-packing houses. In trucker slang they are often called "bull haulers." Before these trucks became common, livestock had to be driven hundreds of miles on foot—to railroad depots or packing centers. Many animals died on the way, and the farmers had to pay high railway freight charges. Now big livestock trucks can haul livestock easily. The slatted sides let in plenty of fresh air.

Beverage Trucks seem to be everywhere nowadays. They supply canned and bottled beverages to stores and restaurants. The trucks come in different sizes. They are specially designed to carry their fragile cargo safely. This big carrier has five compartments on each side of the truck. These compartments are just the right size to hold cases of bottles or cans. They keep the bottles from bouncing around and breaking when the truck gives a sudden shake or jolt.

Each compartment has its own door that slides up so the driver can get to the cases he needs at each stop. There is also a place behind the rear wheel to store a hand cart. The driver will need this to push the heavy cases into the store. Often he picks up empty bottles and cans at the store and loads them into his truck in plastic bags to take back to the manufacturer.

Sanitation Trucks help to keep our towns and cities clean. This sanitation truck is an advanced one-man side loader. As the truck moves slowly down the street, a sanitation worker picks up people's garbage and throws it into the part of the truck called the hopper. Then the worker pulls a lever, starting a special motor that drives a big press inside the hopper. This press crushes the garbage and pushes it toward the back of the truck. The garbage is squeezed together tightly so the truck can haul a bigger load.

Street Cleaners also help to keep streets clean. These amazing motorized sweepers travel alongside the curb. Their revolving brushes scoop up all the dirt and trash that is littering the street. At the same time, little streams of water shoot down onto the pavement to keep dust from flying into the air.

Lattice Boom Truck Cranes are taller than they are long—at least when their boom is fully extended. They are very useful in the construction of tall buildings. They can lift heavy loads such as steel girders. The driver sits in a cab at the front of the truck. The crane operator has his own cab at the rear.

The truck crane in this picture has eight wheels and can lift up to 140 tons (the weight of about twenty-three male African elephants). Its boom extends 230 feet. When the boom lifts a heavy load, the truck has to have a special weight at its front to keep from toppling over. There are also two "feet," called outriggers, on each side of the truck. The outriggers help to balance the truck when it is hoisting its load. Cranes can travel on highways, but they are usually taken apart and loaded onto other trucks when they travel from one building site to another.

Cherry Pickers lift people instead of steel girders. They have a long mechanical arm that can rise into the air. At the end of the arm is a metal bucket, large enough to hold a person. By using one of these cherry pickers or bucket trucks, an electric company can repair electric wires at the top of a tall pole. Workers can replace burned-out bulbs in overhead street lights.

Dump Trucks carry loads of dirt, sand, gravel, or rocks. Early trucks that carried loose materials had to have their loads shoveled out by workmen. Modern dump trucks are automatic. The driver pulls one lever, and the tailgate unlocks. The driver pulls another lever, and long hydraulic rams or pumps lift the end of the dump box. The load tumbles out. In no time at all the dump truck has done the work of several workers with shovels.

Concrete Mixers deliver freshly mixed concrete right to the place where it is needed. The concrete is mixed while the truck travels. The truck has a water tank and a large barrel-shaped drum that carries the concrete mixture, usually sand, cement, and gravel. As the truck travels along the highway, a motor keeps the drum turning while water from the water tank is fed into the drum. By the time the concrete mixer has arrived at the construction site, the concrete is ready. The mixture pours down a chute into molds set up to shape the concrete. The concrete mixer can travel over rough ground as well as on highways.

Off-Road Dump Trucks are built to drive over rough ground. On their heavy-tread, giant tires they can carry extra-heavy loads of rocks or coal. Many of them spend all their time working at construction sites. Often these off-road vehicles are too heavy to travel on a highway. They would crack the pavement. The wheels are sometimes twice as tall as the drivers.

Pole Trailers transport huge logs from the forest to the lumber mill, where they are cut into boards. Years ago, lumbermen had to float their logs down a river to the mills. Then they began to use railroads. Now big logging trucks like the one below can carry logs to the sawmill directly from the place where the trees are cut.

The pole trailer does not have any floor or platform. Instead, a pole runs from the front end of the trailer to its back wheels. Big u-shaped beams at the front and back hold the logs in place. Strong steel chains keep the logs from falling off. Enormous **log-stacking machines** load the logs onto the trailer. Their curved tusks and straight forks are attached to a lifting mast. They can open up and grasp a stack of logs 15 or 16 feet high.

Pumpers are fire trucks that carry a pump and hoses and nozzles of several sizes. They also have built-in water tanks. The fire fighters can use this emergency water supply while they are attaching other hoses to fire hydrants or a local water supply. The powerful pumps can pump several hundred gallons of water per minute.

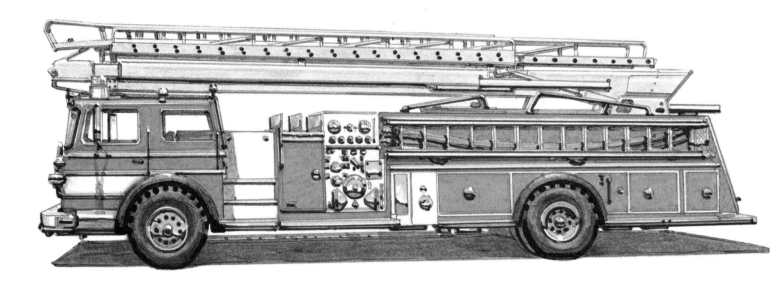

Ladder Trucks carry ladders and rescue equipment—axes, torches, crowbars, stretchers, and first-aid kits. On an aerial ladder truck a long extension ladder rises right up out of the truck. Because this ladder is mounted on a turntable and worked by a motor, it can be moved in any direction by controls in the truck. On the biggest trucks the ladder can stretch up to 100 feet (about eight stories high). A built-in hose runs the length of the ladder. These trucks also carry smaller, portable ladders.

Tow Trucks rescue cars or trucks that have been in accidents or are not running properly. Tow trucks—also called wreckers—come in different sizes. They all have a strong crane at the rear of the truck. Cables with hooks run over a boom and fasten to the front of the wrecked vehicle. At the other end, the cables are fastened to a hoisting machine called a winch. The winch reels the cables up, just like a fishing-rod line, lifting the front wheels of the towed vehicle off the ground. Sometimes tow trucks remove cars that are parked where they shouldn't be.

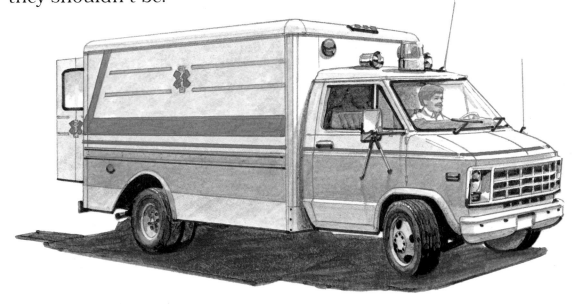

Ambulances transport people who are sick or who have been hurt in an accident. These emergency trucks are specially designed vans with a door at the rear so the patient can be moved in or out on a stretcher. They are often painted with crosses and other special markings. As ambulances race down the street, their loud sirens and flashing lights warn other drivers that they are coming. Many larger ambulances carry emergency equipment such as bandages, oxygen masks, and breathing machines. Trained workers called paramedics often travel with the patient.

Scissors Trucks are used to lift people and things into the air. The body of the truck can be raised by scissors-like legs under the truck bed. These high-lift trucks are usually found at airports, where they are used to load food into passenger planes. Since the plane door is higher than the truck, the truck body rises up to the level of the door. Then the airport workers move the food right into the plane. This is much easier than trying to carry the heavy supplies up a ladder or stairway.

Snowblowers are also useful at airports. They quickly clear the snow off runways and clear out roads leading to and from the terminals. A large snowblower can blow as much as 50 tons of snow per minute! That is the weight of about fifty cars. This truck has rotary ribbon blades that break up the snow. A fan blows the snow through a spout facing out. The road is clear in no time.

Motor Homes are special trucks built for people to live in when they go on vacation or travel around the country. These trucks hold everything a family needs for daily living—beds, refrigerator, stove, shower, toilet, and comfortable chairs. This motor home has bunks over the cab, as well as a large double bed at the rear of the trailer.

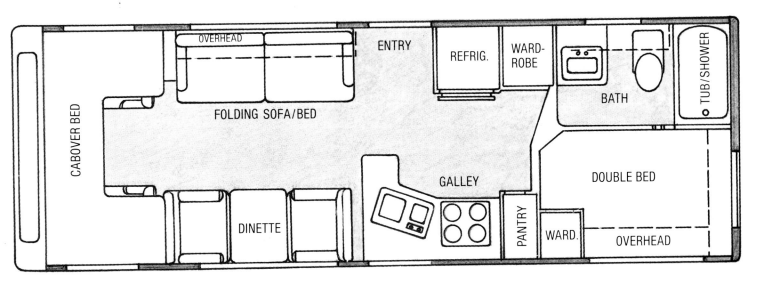

Motor Home Floor Plan

Motor homes come in many sizes. They usually have air conditioners and special heating units. Many include color television and microwave ovens. In a motor home you can enjoy all the conveniences of home while "on the road."

Inside a Motor Home

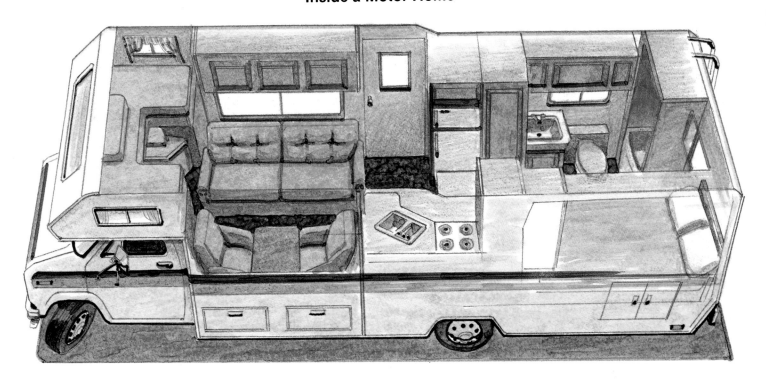

A **Crawler Transporter** is used by the National Aeronautics and Space Administration (NASA) for carrying a space shuttle and its launching platform. It is probably the largest land vehicle in the world. It is also the slowest. The monster crawler transporter is 114 feet wide and 131 feet long—bigger than a basketball court. When fully loaded, it weighs 17 million pounds and creeps along at a speed of just 1 mile an hour.

The amazing crawler transporter travels from the assembly building to the launch pad on its own special "crawlerway." The crawlerway is nearly as wide as an eight-lane superhighway. (Imagine eight cars traveling side by side down an enormous roadway!) At the pad, the launching platform and space shuttle are jacked up on six 22-foot-high support stands. As soon as everything is securely in place, the crawler transporter backs out and slowly creeps away.

Trucks That Perform Special Services

GLASS TRUCK

BOOKMOBILE

VENDOR TRUCK

MAIL TRUCK

BREAD TRUCK

ARMORED TRUCK